Take up Badminton

Take up Sport

Titles in this series currently available or shortly to be
published:

Take up Badminton

Principal contributor:
Barbara M. Jones
County Coach

SPRINGFIELD BOOKS LIMITED

Copyright © Springfield Books Limited and White Line Press 1989

ISBN 0 947655 60 3

First published 1989 by
Springfield Books Limited
Springfield House, Norman Road, Denby Dale, Huddersfield HD8 8TH

Reprinted 1991

Edited, designed and produced by
White Line Press
60 Bradford Road, Stanningley, Leeds LS28 6EF

Editors: Noel Whittall and Philip Gardner
Design: Krystyna Hewitt
Diagrams: Steve Beaumont, Chadwick Studio and IT Design Associates

Printed and bound in Hong Kong

Photographic credits
All photographs (including cover) by Peter Richardson
Illustration page 6: Wimbledon Lawn Tennis Museum

Contents

The early days of badminton in India: the high net, and the possibility of having more than two players on each side, would have made it very different from the modern game

1

Introduction

Origins of the sport

The game of badminton is based on the ancient game of *shuttlecock and battledore*, which was played as an informal indoor or outdoor game, and by children at annual festivals. This involved simply hitting a feathered missile from one player to another, and is thought to date back to the middle ages.

Badminton takes its name from Badminton House, the Duke of Beaufort's stately home in Gloucestershire. There, one rainy day in the late 1860s, a party of adults were seeking a diversion, and adapted the old children's game by stringing up a makeshift net over which the shuttlecock had to be hit. Initially the idea was to keep the shuttlecock in the air for as long as possible, simply hitting it to and fro over the net for the fun of it. However, it was not long before players began to make it difficult for those on the other side of the net to make a return, and the modern game was born.

The main area for development after that was India, where badminton became popular among army officers and civil servants, but it soon began to spread in Britain too, and in 1893 the Badminton Association was formed, adopting a uniform set of laws. Badminton has steadily grown worldwide, and the International Badminton Federation was founded in 1934.

A world game

Badminton is now played at many levels throughout the world; it can be a fun game on lawn or beach, or a highly competitive athletic game, played at national and international levels.

More than 90 countries, with representatives from all continents, take part. The International Badminton Federation controls the laws of the game and organises the World Championships. These are for individuals and pairs, while teams compete for the Thomas Cup (men) and the Uber Cup (ladies).

The Badminton Association of England hosts the annual All England Championships, a prestigious tournament dating back to 1899, and still regarded as an unofficial world championship.

Badminton was included in the 1988 Olympic Games in Seoul as an exhibition sport and is included in the official list for the 1992 Games in Barcelona. It is also a popular sport in the Commonwealth Games.

In Britain, most local authorities are involved in organising badminton activities, usually through leisure services, education, recreation or sports departments. Many run classes in sports centres and schools, for beginners and improvers. In some areas, special classes are organised for ethnic groups. Your local sports hall, library or sports shops may also provide information.

Badminton is played in virtually all countries, so wherever you are you should be able to take up the game if you make enquiries with your local sporting authorities. Some useful addresses are included on pages 54–56.

What it's all about

The object of the game is to hit the shuttle over the net so that it lands in your opponent's court before it can be returned.

The shuttle can be hit fast, slow, high, flat or low. You can use the most delicate touch shots or smash it with maximum power.

When the shuttle is returned, a "rally" is started. Rallies can vary in length from two shots to as many as a hundred.

Each rally begins with a stroke known as the *serve.* This gets the shuttle into play, and from then on you will be engaged in a battle to outwit your opponent by using strokes which aim to increase your chances of winning that rally. We'll look at the different techniques a little later.

The commonest ways for you to win the rally are:

● you hit the shuttle onto the ground in your opponent's court

● your opponent makes a mistake and hits the shuttle out of court

● your opponent hits the shuttle into the net

The appeal of badminton

Badminton is enormously popular for a wide variety of reasons:

- Striking a missile with a weapon seems to satisfy a basic natural instinct.

- Badminton can be played by all age groups, from under seven to over seventy.

- It can easily be adapted for youngsters and disabled players, for example by using a shorter court and a lower net.

- It is an excellent way of developing hand−eye coordination through play.

Badminton clothing can be attractive as well as functional. Jill Wallwork is an international badminton player (Lancashire and England)

- It doesn't need too much space, so can be played indoors — a great advantage in many climates.

- The equipment is simple: all it takes to get started is two people, two rackets, a net and a shuttlecock (we'll simply call it the shuttle from now on). Equipment can often be hired or borrowed so that you can try the game.

- Specialist clothing is not essential, but there is a wide range of attractive and fashionable clothing available.

- Boys and girls, men and women, can all play the game together — a great social advantage.

- The game is played all year round, although the formal competitive season in Great Britain is from September to April.

- Play can be singles, level doubles (same sex) or mixed doubles.

- You can compete at a friendly informal level, or progress through the more strenuous route of organised leagues and tournaments.

- Badminton is one of the easiest games to learn.

- Above all, it is great fun to play!

Forehand grip: gently squeeze the racket handle with the finger and thumb

Backhand grip

2
Getting started

Before you spend money on equipment, you should, if possible, get the feel of the game by trying it out. Often you will be able to borrow a racket and a shuttle from a friend. Also, sports centres usually hire out these items for use on their courts.

Wear suitable training shoes (see page 14), and comfortable clothing which allows you to move and stretch with ease.

In a suitable space, where there is no chance of hitting anyone or anything, get the feel of the racket. Hold it lightly between your thumb and fingers, which should spread out along the middle part of the handle.

Practise hitting the shuttle upwards into the air. Watch the shuttle fall back towards the strings of the racket, and hit it repeatedly, counting how many times you do so without a mistake. No doubt you will have a little trouble trying to keep control, so let's look at the best way to hold the racket, before doing any more practice:

There are two sides to the racket head: the *forehand face* and the *backhand face*. You can hit the shuttle with either of them. Try hitting upwards, first on the forehand, and then on the backhand face of the racket.

To keep maximum control, you should change your grip (see photographs opposite) when you change from forehand to backhand.

Check your forehand grip to see if it is correct: the bottom of the "V" formed between your thumb and forefinger should be in line with the edge of the racket head. You should be able to see the "butt" of the racket at the bottom of your hand.

In the backhand grip, your thumb should point towards the "T" or throat of the racket. The pad of your thumb should press lightly on the handle.

Now try a few simple practices with the shuttle before going on court to play a game...

Using the forehand grip, practise hitting the shuttle upwards with the forehand face of the racket. Change

11

to the backhand grip and do the same, using the backhand face of the racket. First try hitting the shuttle high into the air, then hit it more gently so that it stays closer to the racket.

You will notice that, when you are using the forehand grip, it is the palm of your hand which seems to direct the shuttle, whereas with the backhand, it is your thumb.

Next, hold the shuttle by its feathers with the fingers of your free hand. Using an underarm action, hit it forwards over an imaginary net. This is the action you will use when you serve.

Practise hitting the shuttle into a space in front of you

Practise this action both on your forehand and backhand.

In this early practice you should hit the shuttle with a "flat" racket face (see Figure 1). Later on there will be times when you slice across the base of the shuttle with an angled racket face.

Figure 1 Hitting the shuttle with a "flat" racket face (left) and with an angled racket face (right)

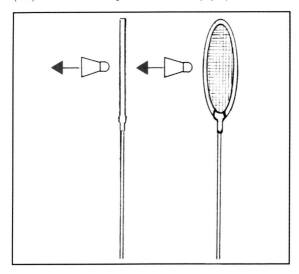

After a little practice you will be able to hit the shuttle in different directions and to various distances. Sometimes it feels as though you are pushing the shuttle; at other times it feels as though you are tapping it. For the push action, keep the hand cocked back at the wrist throughout the stroke; for the tap action, let the hand uncock sharply on impact.

Sometimes it is useful to play with a shortened grip. This gives greater control of the racket head, and is best for some serves and also for shots which are hit from close to the net. For this grip, move your hand nearer to the racket head.

Shortened grip

Once you have done some practice, you can begin to play a form of badminton with your friends. No doubt this will make you want to play more, to play better and to play properly, according to the rules. Read on...

3
Clothing and equipment

Clothing

Look good, feel good, play well is a good philosophy to follow. Take a pride in your appearance and look the part, and you will soon begin to feel like a top player.

Choose clothing which fits comfortably and enables you to move and stretch easily. Most department stores and sports shops sell leisure wear suitable for badminton. Matching shirt and shorts or skirt are attractive, and white is a requirement in some competitions. Some sports halls can be cold, so a sweater is useful — I like the sleeveless type which keeps your body warm but leaves your arms free to work without hindrance. Avoid sloppy sweaters which can get in your way as you play. A tracksuit is worthwhile too, so that you can warm up before play and cool down gradually afterwards.

Your feet will do a great deal of work when you play, so treat them with respect! The game demands constant starts, stops and changes of direction, so do get good sports shoes — some are available which are specially designed for badminton. These are not too heavy and allow flexible movements of the foot while giving enough support and protection during the action.

Replace the shoes as soon as the treads on the soles have begun to wear smooth. Keep the slightly worn ones for use on courts such as those with a carpet-like floor covering.

Fresh, clean socks are vital: the type with a looped pile is particularly long-wearing and comfortable.

If you have long hair, you may need to tie it back or wear a head-band so that it doesn't fall over your eyes and restrict your vision.

Figure 2 The racket

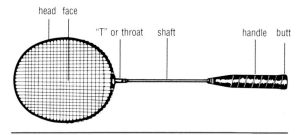

Your racket

Choosing your first racket should be a pleasure: here are some pointers towards picking one which will suit you, but do try out a few before buying if you possibly can.

● The price range is wide, but don't over-economise. Don't fall for a cheap racket with "soggy" strings and a poor grip. On the other hand, don't rush out to buy the most expensive racket there is.

● Ask an experienced player for advice, and go to a reputable shop which specialises in racket sports.

● Hold the racket, feel the weight and the balance. Modern rackets are light in weight — usually about 95–100 grams — and the frames can be made of steel, aluminium, carbon fibre, ceramic, boron, or a combination of some of these.

● Test the tension of the strings with your fingers; they should feel firm to the touch. Strings can be of gut or synthetic material. The synthetics are the best choice for a beginner, because they are usually more hardwearing than gut, and not as expensive.

● The grip is important to your control of the racket. The racket should feel comfortable as you hold it, and you should be able to control it with finger and thumb as you try out the grip changes. Rackets usually come with leather or plastic grips. Some people like to put a towelling grip on the handle, but this can make it feel uncomfortably thick. Eventually, all grips wear away and can become slippery or uncomfortable, so they need replacing from time to time.

● Since modern rackets are extremely light in weight, most young players can manage to play with an adult racket. However, it is important to check that the handle is not too big for the child's hand: as for adults, the fingers and thumb should be able to meet around the grip. If a very young player has difficulty in coping with a full-size racket, smaller models are available.

● Buy a head-cover with your racket, and use it whenever you are not playing. Treat your racket with respect at all times.

● Don't store your racket close to the central-heating radiators, or leave it exposed to sunlight inside a car.

The shuttlecock

There are basically two different types of shuttle: feather and plastic. The feather ones have a cork base covered in kid leather. These are usually the choice for serious competition, and are rather expensive, as well as being easily damaged. Synthetic shuttles are more robust, and will stand a lot more use. Some of them are manufactured with a cork base so that in play they feel similar to the feather shuttles.

The speed at which the shuttle travels is affected by the density of the air. This means that it will fly more freely in a warm hall than in the denser air of a cold one. To compensate for this, shuttles are graded according to speed, the aim being to end up with a standard performance, regardless of where the game is being played. Law 4.4 — see panel — explains how you check that you are using the right grade.

Law 4.4 Shuttle Testing:

1 To test a shuttle, use a full underhand stroke which makes contact with the shuttle over the back boundary line. The shuttle shall be hit at an upward angle and in a direction parallel to the side lines.

2 A shuttle of correct pace will land not less than 530 mm and not more than 990 mm short of the other back boundary line.

In simple terms, the shuttle should land within nine inches (23 cm) either side of the doubles back service line after being struck as described.

Feather shuttles are graded by number, 77 being a slow one and 82 the fastest. Synthetic shuttles sometimes have their speed indicated by a green, blue or red band, denoting slow, medium or fast.

Don't worry too much about whether the shuttle is exactly the right speed; it's not likely to be far out, and you may as well get on with enjoying the game!

Full-size and junior rackets

Synthetic shuttles and feather ones

4

The court

The playing area is a rectangular court marked out as shown in the diagram. The lines should be 1½ in wide (38 mm). The court is divided across the centre by a net. This is suspended from posts at the sides of the court, and should be 5 ft (1.52 m) high at the centre and 5 ft 1 in (1.55 m) high at the sides.

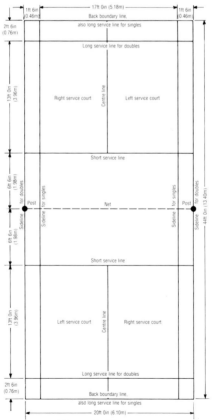

Figure 3 The court

You will see that the court is marked out for both doubles and singles play. The singles game uses the whole length of the court, but the side tramlines are excluded. Note how the shuttle can go right up to the outside edge of the back boundary line during a singles service.

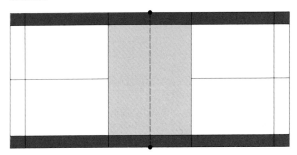

Figure 4 The singles court. The solid coloured area is out for the whole of the game; the area between the net and the front service line (coloured tint) is out for service but in for all other parts of the game

During normal play in the doubles game, the whole court, including the side tramlines, is used. However, the area between the back tramlines is "out" during service.

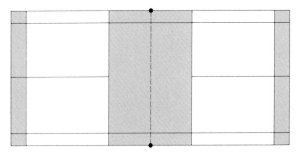

Figure 5 The doubles court. The coloured tint areas are out for service but the whole court is in for all other parts of the game

In all games, the area between the net and the front service line is "out" for service but "in" at all other times during the game. Of course, you don't know for certain whether a service would be "in" or "out" unless it touches the ground: judging whether to leave a marginal serve is one of the key skills of the game.

Short badminton, a junior version of the game played on a smaller court, is described in chapter 9.

5

Playing the game

Starting play

There are various ways to decide how the game will be started. These are the most popular:

- Toss a coin — heads or tails

- Spin a racket — rough or smooth according to the loops at the base of the strings

- Throw the shuttle upwards into the air — if it lands with the base pointing towards you, you have first choice

Serving and scoring

Whoever wins the toss can choose *either* whether to serve first, *or* to begin play at one particular end of the court. The scoring system in badminton is similar to that of volleyball or squash, in that *only the serving side can score a point*, so it is usual for the winner of the toss to choose to serve first. You keep on serving until you lose a rally. There are rules for where you serve *from*, and where you serve *to*, and we will look at them all in turn.

> The expression *rally* is used to indicate any period of play between serves; it does not have to be a long series of shots.

Singles

In singles, you start by serving from the right-hand court, and you must serve to the court diagonally opposite. If you win that point, the next serve is from the left-hand court, and so on.

If your opponent wins the rally, but you served, it's *service over* and your opponent becomes the server. When this happens, the score remains the same: no one scores a point.

You serve from the right-hand court when your score is 0, 2, 4, 6 etc (even numbers) and from the left-hand court at 1, 3, 5, 7 etc (odd numbers).

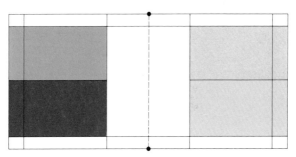

Figure 6 The serving courts and corresponding receiving courts (tint of the same colour)

In girls' and ladies' singles, a game is played up to eleven points – i.e. the first player to reach eleven points wins. Boys and men play up to fifteen points, and doubles games are played to fifteen points too.

← *Spinning a racket to decide who has first choice*

Doubles

At first, you have to keep your wits about you to work out whose turn it is to serve in a doubles game; here are the rules. We will imagine that your side have won the toss, and you are to serve first. Not unreasonably, you are referred to as the *first server.*

As first server, you have to start from your right-hand court. You serve diagonally across the net to the *first receiver* on the other side.

If your side fails to win this first point, the right to serve goes to the player who was first receiver on the other side. *It is only after the first service of each game that the right to serve passes to the other side on the loss of the first rally.* For the rest of the game, the serve passes to your partner before going to your opponents.

If you serve and win the rally, your side scores a point and you continue to serve, but from the other service court, diagonally to the *second receiver.*

If you serve and lose the rally (other than the first rally of the game), your partner — the *second server* — serves likewise from the opposite court, diagonally to the next receiver. Then, when the second server loses a rally, your opponents take over the service.

Law 14: Service Court Errors

14.1 A service court error has been made when a player:

1 has served out of turn;

2 has served from the wrong service court; or

3 standing in the wrong service court, was prepared to receive the service and it has been delivered.

14.2 When a service court error has been made, then:

1 if the error is discovered before the next service is delivered, it is a "let" unless only one side was at fault and lost the rally, in which case the error shall not be corrected.

2 if the error is not discovered before the next service is delivered, the error shall not be corrected.

14.3 If there is a "let" because of a service court error, the rally is replayed with the error corrected.

14.4 If a service court error is not to be corrected, play in that game shall proceed without changing the players' new service courts (nor, when relevant, the new order of serving).

Even experienced players occasionally find that they are serving out of sequence, and the official Laws of Badminton lay down procedures for dealing with this (see panel). If you do get into a tangle, you can sort it out by remembering the following:

● The player in the right-hand court always begins serving, and then changes to the left-hand court and back to the right-hand court with each serve.

● If, at the beginning of the game, you are *first server* or *first receiver*, you should always be in the *right*-hand court at the start of each rally when your side's score is an *even number*.

● After your second server has lost the right to serve, the call is *service over*, and the other side's first server continues the game.

Changing ends

In both singles and doubles play, a match is decided by the best of three games. At the end of the first game, you change ends and the winners serve. If, after two games, the result is one game each, a third game is played. You should change ends again after the second game, and half-way through the third — that is:

● if you are playing an 11-point game, change when the leading score reaches 6

● in a 15-point game, change when the leading score reaches 8

If you forget to change ends, do so as soon as you realise that this has happened, and play on.

Setting

In a game to fifteen points, if the score is 13–13, the side which reached that score first has the choice of choosing either:

"*to play straight through please*", to the normal score of fifteen points;

or "*to set, please*", which extends the game.

If a side decides to *set* at 13–13, the game is restarted at 0–0 and is played up to five points. In doubles, the serving side continues the serving pattern reached at 13–13.

Setting is also permitted at 14–14, in which case the resumed play is for a further three points.

Note that it is the *first* side to 13 or 14 points which has the option of *setting*. Even if no decision was taken to *set* at 13–13 points, it is still permitted at 14–14.

In women's games, played to eleven points, *setting* is permitted at 9–9, in which case a further three points are played, or at 10–10, for a further two points.

A player declining to take the first opportunity of *setting* may still do so if the opportunity arises again.

Handicap competitions

Handicapping is quite popular in badminton. It gives players of mixed ability the opportunity to play together by giving the less-accomplished player an advantage at the start. For example, a good player may have to start with a score of −4, or the less skilled may start at +6.

Setting is not allowed in handicap competitions.

Laws of serving

When serving, you must:

● Stand completely inside your own service area, without touching any of the lines.

● Keep some part of *both* feet stationary and in contact with the court.

● Serve, using only one forward action of the racket.

● Strike the base of the shuttle with the racket. At the moment of striking, no part of the shuttle may be above your waist.

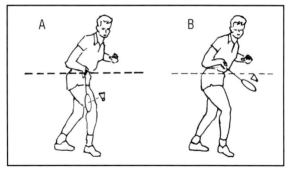

Figure 7 When serving, no part of the shuttle may be above your waist: A is clearly legal; B, where the top of the shuttle is at waist height, is only just legal

● Ensure that all of the racket head is completely below the lowest point of your hand at the moment of striking the shuttle. This means you must serve underarm.

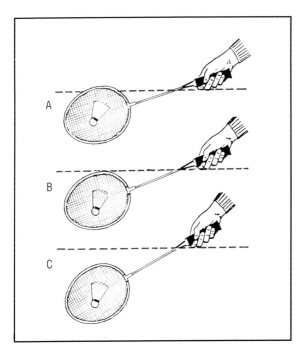

Figure 8 The racket head must be completely below the lowest point of your hand as you strike the shuttle. A is a fault; B, the borderline case, is also a fault; C is correct.

- Once the receiver is in position, you must not deliberately delay serving so as to gain an unfair advantage.
- In doubles, your partner can stand anywhere, providing he or she does not obstruct the receiver's view of the shuttle and does not distract the receiving side.

Laws of receiving service

There are rules for receiving too! You must:

- Stand in the area of the court diagonally opposite the service court, without touching any part of the boundary lines.
- Keep some part of *both* feet stationary and in contact with the court until the shuttle is hit by the server.
- Not make any movement to deliberately distract the server.

- Not deliberately delay so as to gain an unfair advantage over the server.

- If you attempt to return the service, you are considered to have been ready.

- In doubles, your partner can stand anywhere, providing he or she does not obstruct or distract the server in any way.

Faults

Once the shuttle is in play, there are a number of ways the rally can be lost:

- Failing to return the shuttle to the court on the opponent's side of the net.

- Catching or slinging the shuttle with the racket.

- Hitting the shuttle more than once with separate strokes.

- Making contact with the shuttle before it has crossed the net. (The racket can follow-through over the net after contact with the shuttle, provided the racket does not touch the net).

- Contacting the posts or net other than with the shuttle.

- Invading the opponent's territory with foot, body or racket; e.g. standing with your foot under the net. The follow-through, mentioned above, is an exception to this rule.

- Touching the shuttle when it is in play other than with the racket.

- Failing to strike the shuttle when serving.

It is not a fault if the shuttle touches the net cord as it passes over the top of the net.

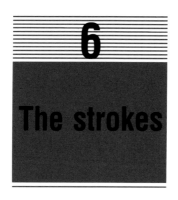

6

The strokes

A stroke is a particular technique for hitting the shuttle over the net. The pathway along which the shuttle travels — which is different for each stroke — is called its *trajectory*.

Adopting the defensive ready position

At the start of each stroke, it is essential to have your hand cocked backwards. You can play the stroke with an overarm, underarm or sidearm racket action, except for the serve, which has to be underarm. Each action is completed by what feels like a "push", a "tap" or a "whip" with the hand. Each stroke you play is a move in the game. This is one reason why badminton is sometimes referred to as "physical chess".

Ready position

It is no use knowing all the strokes if you are not able to play them in time. This is why you need to develop the habit of taking up a *ready* position automatically between shots (see photo on page 27).

The racket head is in front of your body, pointing slightly upwards, with your hand cocked back. Be alert, ready to react quickly.

The leg on the same side of your body as your racket hand is referred to as your *racket leg.*

Playing the strokes

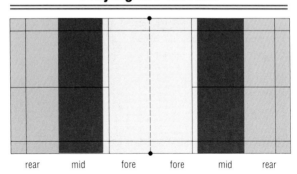

| rear | mid | fore | fore | mid | rear |

Figure 9 To help describe the shots, the court is divided into three approximately equal parts: the rearcourt, midcourt and forecourt

Low serve

Grip: forehand or backhand

Action: underarm push

Played from: behind the front service line

Played to: on or beyond the diagonally-opposite front service line

Shuttle trajectory

Figure 10

Tips on playing the stroke

- Stand in a comfortable, balanced position.
- Keep the hand cocked back throughout the stroke. Stay relaxed.
- Push the shuttle with the racket face.
- Try to make the shuttle "skim" the tape.
- Try the shortened grip.

Use in the game: to get the rally started without giving your opponent an advantage

Other points: check the laws of serving (page 24)

Flick serve

Grip: forehand or backhand

Action: underarm tap

Played from: behind the front service line

Played to: past or over the receiver's racket

Shuttle trajectory

Figure 11 Here the shuttle is shown landing in the doubles service court

Tips on playing the stroke

- Stand in a comfortable, balanced position.
- Give the impression that that you are going to "push" the shuttle as in the low serve, but use the "tap" action for the final part of the stroke.

Use in the game: to deceive and keep at bay an opponent who is threatening your low serve.

Other points: check the laws of serving

High serve

Grip: forehand

Action: underarm whip

Played from: two to three feet (750–900 mm) behind the front service line

Played to: diagonally opposite service court, but *as far back as possible*, while remaining "in".

Shuttle trajectory

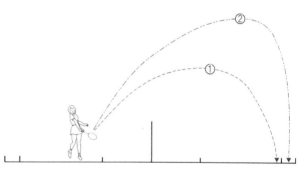

Figure 12 The high doubles serve (1) and high singles serve (2)

Tips on playing the stroke

Stand slightly sideways on, feet comfortably apart. Your racket leg should be the leg furthest back. Take your arm and racket back as for a big underarm throw. Before the throw begins, cock your hand back so that the racket head points upwards. Hold the shuttle by the feathers with your arm reaching slightly out in front of you. Try to release the shuttle from the same place each time you serve. Get the feeling of throwing the racket head at the shuttle. Release the shuttle and hit it with the flat face of the racket, finishing with a "whip" action. To control the direction, let your racket head follow the line of flight of the shuttle.

Use in the game: to move your opponent as far back in court as possible, thus creating a space in the forecourt

Other points: check the laws of serving

Lob

The lob is sometimes called the *underarm clear*.

Grip: forehand or backhand
Action: underarm whip or tap
Played from: the forecourt, below net height
Played to: the opponent's rearcourt

Shuttle trajectory

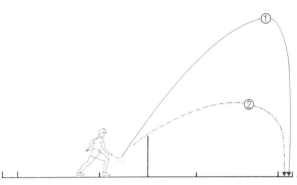

Figure 13 The defensive lob (1) and attacking lob (2)

Tips on playing the stroke
Step towards the shuttle with your racket leg. Feel as though you are throwing your racket head at the shuttle. Make full use of your hand to produce a "whip" action, as in the high serve. Maintain balance throughout the stroke, and watch the shuttle carefully.

Use in the game
Lob very high when you need to make time for yourself. It should give you time to get back to your base before your opponent hits the shuttle. A flatter lob can be used to beat an opponent who is in or moving towards the forecourt. This is usually played with a tap action.

Forehand clear

Grip: forehand
Action: overarm whip
Played from: the rearcourt, when the shuttle is high
Played to: the opponent's rearcourt

Shuttle trajectory

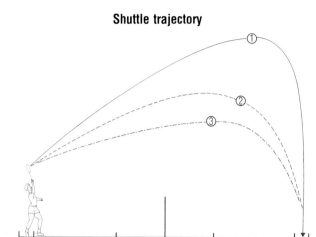

Figure 14 The defensive clear (1), the standard clear (2) and the attacking clear (3)

Tips on playing the stroke

Stand sideways-on, nicely balanced, with your racket leg back. Get right behind the shuttle and use a strong throwing action, as if you are going to throw your racket high and forwards through the air. Let your hand uncock with a "whip" action as you hit through the shuttle.

For improved style and to aid balance, point your free hand at the shuttle before you play the stroke.

Use in the game

● Create time for yourself by hitting the clear with a high trajectory.

● You can also create problems for your opponents by hitting the clear with a flatter trajectory, usually after you have lured them towards the forecourt.

Backhand clear

This is a more advanced shot. It may require the use of the "multi-purpose" grip.

Grip: backhand or multi-purpose

Action: backhand tap

Played from: the rearcourt, when the shuttle is high

Played to: the opponent's rearcourt

Shuttle trajectory

The shuttle takes the same path as in the forehand clear.

The multi-purpose grip

Tips on playing the stroke
Stay relaxed. Reach to contact the shuttle at a comfortable distance from the body. Watch the shuttle carefully, and tap it on its way.

Use in the game: for use against a shuttle which is going past you, high towards your backhand corner.

Overhead backhand

Other points

If you are a beginner, you will probably be more successful playing this as a "round the head" stroke. To do this, you reach high behind your head, across to your non-racket side. Hit with the *forehand* face of your racket.

Steve Baddeley plays a round-the-head stroke

Forehand smash

Grip: forehand

Action: overarm throw

Played from: high in the midcourt or rearcourt

Played to: downwards into the opponent's court

> The smash and the dropshot can also be played with round-the-head or backhand actions.

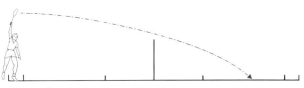

Figure 15

Tips on playing the stroke

Get behind the shuttle, with your body sideways on as for the clear. Use the same whip action, but meet the shuttle further out in front of your body than in the clear.

Use in the game

● To play a winning shot.

● To force your opponent to play a weak reply.

Other points

Make all your overhead strokes *look* like the smash, so that you can then deceive your opponent with alternative shots.

Forehand dropshot

Grip: forehand

Action: overarm push or tap

Played from: high in the rearcourt or midcourt

Played to: the forecourt or the midcourt

Shuttle trajectory

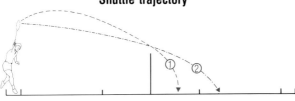

Figure 16 The slow dropshot (1) and the fast dropshot (2)

Tips on playing the stroke

Give the impression that you are going to smash; at the last moment, "push" or "tap" the shuttle.

Use in the game: to make your opponent play a shot from the forecourt, or from close to the floor in the midcourt.

Drives

Grip: forehand or backhand

Action: sideways whip or tap

Played from: midcourt

Played to: midcourt or rearcourt

Shuttle trajectory

Figure 17

Tips on playing the stroke

Point your racket foot towards the shuttle. Imagine you are throwing a stone to skim across the surface of the water. Use the same "whip" action to hit the shuttle so that it skims across the top of the net.

Use in the game: to play a shot which keeps you on the attack when you are unable to hit a downwards shot.

Other points

● A variation on the drive is to use a "tap" action instead of a "whip" action.

● Another side-arm shot is a "push" to your opponent's forecourt or midcourt.

Net kill

This is a downward net shot.

Grip: forehand or backhand

Action: overarm tap

Played from: forecourt (above net height)

Played to: midcourt

Shuttle trajectory

Figure 18

Tips on playing the stroke

Try the shortened grip. Stand with your racket foot forwards. Hold the racket head above net height with your hand cocked back. Tap the shuttle down towards the floor in your opponent's court.

Use in the game

● To play a winning shot.

● To force a weak reply.

Other points: remember that the racket must not touch the net or invade your opponent's territory (except in the follow-through) — see page 26.

Upward net shot

This is sometimes called the *hairpin net shot*.

Grip: forehand or backhand

Action: underarm push

Played from: below net height in the forecourt

Played to: opponent's forecourt

Shuttle trajectory

Figure 19

Tips on playing the stroke

Have your racket leg forward, and meet the shuttle with the racket as close to the top of the net as possible. Turn the racket face to push the shuttle upwards.

Use in the game: to return the shuttle close to the net so as to make replies difficult for your opponent.

Stroke troubleshooting

Beginners often experience problems with certain techniques of the game. Don't get disheartened! Here are ways of overcoming two of the common snags:

Poor overhead throwing action

Some people find that they can't get enough freedom into this action. You need to feel as though you are throwing the head of your racket at a high target in front of you. You need to get it moving fast enough to hear a definite swish as the air whistles through the strings. To help you get the feel of the throwing action, practise throwing a small ball overarm at a high target. Inside the badminton hall you can practise with a soft sponge ball or a shuttle; then try a few "shadow" strokes, without a shuttle, before trying the real thing again.

Once you have got used to the free wrist action of the overhead throw, you will easily be able to adapt it for sideways action too.

Backhand inaccuracy

Beginners tend to aim the back of their hand at the shuttle during backhand strokes, resulting in weak shots. The correct method is to aim the *side* of your hand and racket at the shuttle, karate style, finishing up with a rapid turn of the wrist to bring the racket face square a moment before contacting the shuttle.

Everyone can benefit from a good coaching session

38

7

Improving your game

It's better to start off with good habits than to try to change bad habits later, so seek coaching advice from the beginning if you can.

Most local authorities organise teaching classes for beginners and improvers, and you should not have much difficulty in finding these. Your local public library will probably be able to give you information, and many sports centres hold badminton classes and coaching sessions.

Helping yourself

Whenever possible, watch better players, either live or on television or video. Don't simply concentrate on winning or losing, but observe how the experts constantly play for position. This will soon help you with your own tactics and positioning on court.

You can also learn a lot by asking the better players in your area for advice, but be prepared to help yourself as well.

Good basics are the key to success in all sports. The fundamentals of badminton are good racket and body skills.

The aim of your practice should be to gain the ability to:

- Play all the basic strokes

- Change, at speed, to the appropriate grip to perform the stroke

- Be in balance to play each stroke and recover in time for the next stroke

- Have the racket in the "ready" position between strokes (see page 28)

- Watch the shuttle, particularly at the moment of contact

- Move fluently around the court

Solo practice

The best form of practice is to play the game or to rally with a partner, but fortunately there are also some worthwhile routines you can practise on your own. Try these:

Grip changes

Learn to change grip, from forehand to backhand and back again, really fast! There is only one way to master this — efficient practice. Use your thumb and forefinger to rotate the racket from one grip to another.

It is rather like learning to play a musical instrument — your fingers may feel clumsy at first, but patience and determination soon pay dividends.

Racket head control

Hitting an old shuttle against a wall is a good way of developing control of the racket head. The practice will be even more effective if you can show the height of the net with a chalk line, or a length of string, 5 feet above the ground.

Decide on a stroke, then set yourself goals. Using the simple controlled-push action, hitting straight, you could try a programme like this:

● 10 forehand, then 10 backhand — practise straight and diagonal hitting

● 20, alternating forehand and backhand

Work on the basic shots first. Once you can do them accurately with the push action, build up speed by working on the tap action. When you get out on court again you will find that the ability to move the racket head really fast will make a great difference to the way you can respond.

Hitting a shuttle against a wall is an effective practice at all levels of play.

Serving practice

This is easier if you have a number of shuttles, so that you can repeat your serve without having to retrieve them all the time. Practise the different types of serve, using forehand and backhand, and set out one or two targets for practising serves of different lengths. You could use your racket-head cover as the target.

You can also practise other strokes by hitting the shuttle into the air and then making an overhead shot.

Practices with a partner

Here is a selection of drills to use when you are able to practise with a partner. The first three drills are ideal for use where both of you are of similar ability; the later ones are most effective if your partner is more experienced. Whatever the case, you will find that partner practices will rapidly help you to improve your skills and understanding of the game.

For the first three drills, stand in the middle of one half-court — it doesn't matter whether it is the right or left — with your partner opposite you on the other side of the net.

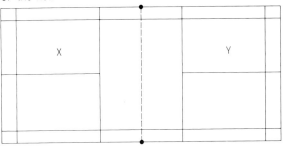

Figure 20 Approximate positions for the all-strokes rally (practice 1) between player X and partner Y

1 All-strokes rally

Try hitting the shuttle between you and your partner, using underarm and overarm actions; vary the strokes, hitting the shuttle forwards, upwards and downwards. Sometimes you will need to use a sideways hitting action (see photo on page 42).

Aim to keep the rally going so that you develop the use of the forehand face and the backhand face of the racket, changing to the appropriate grip. Vary the pace at which you hit the shuttle by using the push and the tap actions. Remember to look at the shuttle, and be aware of the angle of the racket face. On the forehand, feel how the palm of your hand is directing the shuttle, and on the backhand, feel how the thumb does this.

Once you can keep the rally going continuously, with control and accuracy, you can occasionally let the racket head follow the shuttle with a fast "whip" action. This will result in the shuttle travelling faster and further, and it may "beat" your partner, causing the rally to end. If this happens, return to your original positions on court and re-start the practice.

Practise the sideways hitting action

2 Pushing rally
Serve the shuttle low over the net, using a push action. Develop a "pushing" rally in which you both improve your skills and gain confidence in keeping the shuttle low over the net in the forecourt.

3 Net kill rally
Stand on the centre of the front service line in the position to play the net kill; your partner should be just in front of the doubles back service line. Tap the shuttle down towards the feet of your partner, who uses an underarm action to return the shuttle to just above the net, so that you can keep the rally going to improve your control and technique.

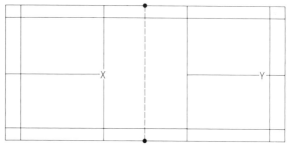

Figure 21 Approximate positions for the net kill rally (practice 3) between player X and partner Y

Stroke-improving drills

The next three drills are aimed at polishing up your stroke technique. Your partner acts as "feeder", placing the shuttle in just the right position for you to respond.

4 Long shots
Stand just in front of the back double serving line and get your partner to serve a shuttle high towards you. As the serve is struck, move to get behind the shuttle. Practise ten separate clears, then ten dropshots, then ten smashes.

The value of the practice does not lie in the number of shuttles you hit, but in the number of quality strokes you make to hit accurate shots.

5 Drives and pushes
Now move to the midcourt to practise your drives and pushes.

6 Net shots
From the forecourt, practise net kills, net shots and lobs.

Practise the strokes for both forehand and backhand. Once you can perform them with accuracy and consistency, you need to think about making your practices more relevant to the game. The next group of drills focuses on this by linking strokes and movement on court. Your partner has to feed the shuttles to you in a sequence which draws you from your base in the midcourt to the rearcourt, then back to the midcourt, then to the forecourt, and so on.

You must choose the best shots to use for the part of the court you are sent to. Once you can perform these skills accurately and consistently, go on to practice sessions which keep the action continuous.

7 Drops and pushes
Get your partner to serve a high shuttle towards the rearcourt. Move from your base to the rearcourt to hit an accurate dropshot down to your partner, who then pushes the shuttle back low over the net towards your midcourt base. You push the shuttle back low to your partner, who lobs it high to the rearcourt, and so the practice continues. (See Fig. 22 overleaf.)

8 Return to base
You hit a deep, high serve to your partner's back boundary line, and then take up your base position in the midcourt. Your partner lures you off base with a dropshot well to the side of either your forehand or

Figure 22 Approximate positions for drops and pushes (practice 7) between player X on base and partner Y in starting position

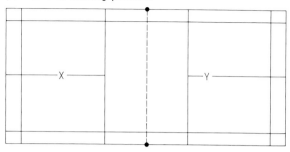

backhand: you respond with a high and accurate lob to the back boundary and return to base immediately. After each shot, you should aim to be back on your base before your partner strikes the shuttle.

This linking together of strokes and movement in a known pattern or sequence is usually called a "fixed routine". These work best if the feeder operates from a pre-determined area of court, such as the rearcourt, and feeds in a fixed pattern to the player, who practises moving and hitting.

Because a sequence should be made up from a logical pattern of strokes which form part of a game, you can see why it is better if your partner is quite experienced. With a good feeder, you will develop skill in hitting as well as efficient control of your movement around the entire court.

Make sure that you use a variety of sequence practices, so that you develop forehand, backhand and round-the-head strokes at high, low and medium height. Allow enough practice time to learn how to use these shots, both straight and cross-court, from any position on court to any area on the other side of the net.

9 Random sequence

This routine will really keep you on your toes: it calls for skill on behalf of the feeder, who has to keep up the rally by sending a series of shots to all areas of your court. They have to be placed so that you can *just* reach them to keep the rally going. Your shot has to return the shuttle to the feeder, *not* to beat him or her! The emphasis is on movement, and you will always have to concentrate on getting back to base ready to position yourself for the next shot. This type of practice can be physically demanding. Build up skill and fitness together by gradually extending the length of the rally.

By this stage in your practice, your balance will be put to the test as you constantly check your movement and change direction. Keeping a good posture, with your knees slightly bent and your weight on the balls of your feet, will help.

As you gain experience, you can take turns with your partner at being the feeder. This will show you some of the effects that the strokes have on the player. Serving and receiving service should form a regular part of your practice. Rehearse this, as well as other strokes, before the start of a game.

10 Receiving serve

This practice is almost identical to a game situation, except that you can face ten or a dozen serves in succession! If the feeder sends a good variety of serves, you will soon improve your ability to react quickly. Remember always to be in the "ready" position, and to stand where you feel you can move quickly forwards or backwards to hit a reply to a low serve or a flick serve.

Always have the racket up in front of you, ready to strike. You can attempt a "kill" if the serve is not a very good one, but otherwise you should concentrate on returning the shuttle without giving your opponent an advantage.

Receiving serve: poised to react quickly

Shadow badminton

Playing badminton regularly is an excellent way of keeping fit, but you may want to do something extra to get fit in the first place. By practising "shadow badminton" — without a shuttle — you can improve your body skills and your fitness at the same time.

Move around the court as if you were playing a game. Play imaginary shots against "the world champion", and keep up the pressure.

Move fast and smoothly, being as light on your feet as possible. Vary the pace: use walking, running and chassé steps (side steps). Aim to keep your balance at all times, particularly when playing the stroke.

Remember to work from a central base to all parts of the court, returning to your base between each stroke.

For a more realistic practice, your partner can direct you to the areas of the court, making sure that you have to go to rearcourt, midcourt and forecourt areas on both your forehand and backhand sides. When travelling to the rearcourt, you should still keep your partner in sight, just as in a real game.

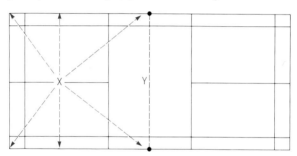

Figure 23 Shadow badminton: your partner Y helps you by directing you to various areas of the court

8

Tactics

Once you have become reasonably fluent with your stroke play, tactics begin to play a really big part in the game. You will already have discovered how it came to be called "physical chess"; here's how you use tactics and strategy as moves to outplay your opponent. The only problem is that your opponent will be trying to do the same to you!

Always remember that you are trying to make your opponent play a weak shot to which you will be able to reply with a strong one or a "kill". Too many beginners try to make every shot a winning shot, instead of negotiating to play a winner.

Singles tactics

Constantly divert the shuttle away from your opponent, always trying to keep him or her moving around the court. Your aim is to make your opponent play a poor return, such as a weak backhand shot from the rearcourt.

If your plan works and forces a mistake or a weak reply which you can hit to the floor, then try it again.

If you are in a difficult situation in the game and your opponent isn't, you need to create time for yourself. Do this by hitting very high, towards the back of the court, preferably near the middle of the back line. From there your opponent will find it difficult to catch you out with awkwardly angled returns. After hitting each high defensive shot, try to get back to your base before your opponent strikes the shuttle.

Doubles tactics

In all types of doubles play, you and your partner should work together as a team to force your opponents to give you the opportunity to hit a winning shot.

Useful negotiating shots are low serves, net shots, pushes to the midcourt, and drives.

Although an ideal player will be skilful in all areas of the court, most will either show greater flair around the net or be more effective with overhead shots. You have to work in such a way that you make the best of your skills together: as well as playing to your opponents' weak areas, try to play to your own strengths.

You will find this much easier if you communicate well with each other. Don't leave it to guesswork! Talk to your partner. Is there a leader in the partnership or is it all a matter of shared responsibility? A quick word on court might change the result of a game which is slipping away from you.

Good shots combined with good teamwork will make you hard to beat!

The positioning for *level* doubles (two men or two women) is usually different from that in *mixed* doubles. We look at level doubles first:

Level doubles

The arrangement known as the *attacking formation* is used when your side is in a position to attack. An imaginary line divides the court across its width, just behind the front service line. One player is responsible for playing shots in the front part of the court (the *front player*), while the other (surprise — the *back player*) goes for all the shuttles that get past the front player.

In the attacking formation, the front player's base is just behind the centre of the front service line, while that of the back player is in the centre of the midcourt.

If your opponents are in an attacking position and able to hit the shuttle down at *you*, you will need to take up a *defensive formation*.

For this, the imaginary line runs lengthways down the centre of the court, and you are responsible for looking after your half. Your base will be in the centre of your half of the midcourt. This formation is often referred to as *sides*.

Mixed doubles

In mixed doubles, the woman usually plays in the front of the court, and her partner takes the shots that get past her. The man should try to hit shots downwards or horizontally, while the woman should play net kills and tight net shots. Both players should be in a good position to push the shuttle low over the net to the midcourt area, just past the front player's area but in front of the back player. This is particularly effective in the side tramlines.

Korean players Park Joo Bong and Lee Sang Bok (the team nearest the camera) illustrate the attacking formation (above) and the defensive formation (below)

The usual formation in mixed doubles is for the women to play in the forecourt and the men in the rearcourt

9

Short badminton

Some players, particularly young children, can find it difficult to hit the shuttle from one end of a full-size court to the other; they may also rapidly become exhausted by trying to move around a large area. For these players, *short badminton* has been devised.

The court size is reduced to:

11 x 4.6 m (36 x 15 ft) for singles
11 x 5.2 m (36 x 17 ft) for doubles

The net can also be lowered to 1.3 m (4 ft 3 in). This reduced net height allows small players to hit down effectively.

On this size of court, young children can have an enjoyable game, and soon begin to appreciate the part that tactics can play.

Short badminton

10

Safety

Badminton is a relatively safe game, and if you take reasonable care there is little risk of injury. Warming up before play *is* important, and will reduce the chances of muscle and joint injury. See the panel on page 52 for a couple of simple stretching exercises which will prepare you for the game, and in the "knock up" on court, play gentle shots at first.

Extra care should be taken in cold halls, where keeping warm between games is important. After a game, put on an extra layer of clothing — a tracksuit is ideal — so that your body will cool down gradually.

Slippery floors can be a hazard, and should be avoided if possible. If you have no choice, you can increase grip by placing a damp cloth at the side of the court so that you can occasionally dampen the soles of your badminton shoes.

In strenuous play, you may get blisters on your feet or hands, so it's worth carrying some plasters in your sports bag.

Hard physical exercise of any type, particularly in hot conditions, can lead to dehydration. Badminton is no exception! Take small quantities of water or diluted soft drinks, both before play and at intervals during play, to prevent this.

Eye injuries do not happen often, but you must be prepared for the possibility. Keep your racket head up, so that you can intercept any shuttle which is coming towards your face. If you are playing near the net in doubles, do not turn round to see what shot your partner is going to hit — it's better to get a shuttle in the neck than in the eye!

Take care to avoid running into anyone when you are practising, and be aware of the danger of hitting your partner with your racket: this can happen if you both go to hit the shuttle at the same time.

If the shuttle is hit onto another court, where play is in progress, wait for an appropriate moment, when play has stopped, to retrieve it.

When leaving your court, remember not to cross too close behind any other court where play is in progress.

Young players should not copy adult training methods. In particular, avoid weight training, which is only suitable for physically mature adults, and needs expert advice.

With sensible preparation and a little care, most accidents can be prevented.

---

1 Twisting tone-up

Sit on the floor with your legs straight. Bend your right knee and put your right foot outside your left knee. Now twist from the waist as far to the right as possible and place your palms on the ground, *keeping your bottom firmly on the floor.* Try to relax your back, and hold the position for a count of ten. Easy. Now change legs and repeat the exercise in the other direction. Now do it all five or ten times...

2 Shoulder stretch

Stand with legs apart and arms in front of you with fingers interlaced and your palms facing away from you. Now, keeping your chin tucked in, steadily raise your arms above your head as far as they will go. Hold for one minute. Swing your arms and shoulders a bit before going on to the next exercise.

11

A social game

Badminton is enjoyed by young children, teenagers, adults and senior citizens alike. Fortunately, courtesy and consideration are still a part of the badminton scene, and we rely on newcomers to keep it that way. Here are some of the courtesies which are observed:

- If someone helps you, whether a friend, parent, teacher or coach, a simple "thank you" will be appreciated. The same applies to your partner and your opponents after a game, no matter what the result is.

- Shaking hands is a recognised courtesy. If you play a game in which you are beaten by a better player, recognise his or her better qualities, and get back to the practice court to improve your own game.

- In doubles, work as a team and never blame your partner.

- If you play competitive badminton, remember to give a word of thanks to the officials and organisers, who usually give their time free of charge.

Badminton is played by people of all age groups

Useful addresses

Great Britain

The Badminton Association of England (BAE) is the governing body of the game in England, and is responsible for promoting the game, organising major events, arranging courses for players at all levels, and training coaches. The BAE publishes the informative magazine *Badminton Now*, as well as other publications, including *The Laws of Badminton* and a diary of events. It also produces instructional videos. The BAE has nine regional officers who coordinate activities in their respective regions, which are based on the Sports Council's regions.

Badminton Association of England (BAE)
National Badminton Centre
Bradwell Road
Loughton Lodge
Milton Keynes MK8 9LA

Tel: 0908 568822

Badminton Union of Ireland (BUI)
The House of Sport
Upper Malone Road
Belfast BT9 5LA

Tel: 0232 661222

English Schools Badminton Association (ESBA)
National Badminton Centre
Bradwell Road
Loughton Lodge
Milton Keynes MK8 9LA

Tel: 0908 568822

The English Schools Badminton Association has a wide range of activities. It runs national championships at under-16, under-14 and under-12 levels, and frequent competitions in the 12-16 age groups. ESBA runs award schemes for pupils (six levels) and teachers. It also provides *ESBA Post*, a magazine and information service for all concerned with junior badminton.

Scottish Badminton Union (SBU)
Cockburn Centre
12–40 Bogmoor Road
Glasgow G51 4FN

Tel: 041-445 1218

Sports Council
16 Upper Woburn Place
London WC1H 0QP

Tel: 01-388 1277

Welsh Badminton Union (WBU)
3rd Floor
3 Westgate Street
Cardiff CF1 1DD

Tel: 0222 22082

Overseas

European Badminton Union
Vluyner Platz 7 & 8
D-4150 Krefeld
Federal Republic of Germany

Tel: 2151 581214

Australian Badminton Association
32 Bird Road
Kalamunda 6076
Western Australia

Canadian Badminton Association
1600 James Naismith Drive
Gloucester
Ontario
K1B 5N4
Canada

China Badminton Association
9 Tiyukuan Road
Beijing
People's Republic of China

Badminton Association of India
Jackson's Hotel
Jabalpur
(MP) 482001
India

Badminton Association of Malaysia
Kompleks Belia Bandaraya
Batu 3½ Jalan Cheras
56000 Kuala Lumpur
Malaysia

New Zealand Badminton Federation
PO Box 11-319
Wellington
New Zealand

Pakistan Badminton Federation
297-A(11) New Muslim Town
Lahore
Pakistan

United States Badminton Association
501 West 6th Street
Papillion
NE 68046-3030
USA

International

International Badminton Federation (IBF)
24 Winchcombe House
Winchcombe Street
Cheltenham
Gloucestershire GL52 2NA

Tel: 0242 517157